Original title:
The Art of Burrowing

Editor: Jessica Elisabeth Luik
Author: Johan Kirsipuu
ISBN HARDBACK: 978-9916-86-523-1
ISBN PAPERBACK: 978-9916-86-524-8

Hollows of Harmony

In the twilight's gentle embrace cool,
Where shadows dance and moonlight rules,
Whispers of night in the air pool,
Crafting dreams from stardust and jewel.

Forests echo the melody pure,
Leaves rustle in harmonious cure,
Crickets chirp their serenade sure,
While owls in wisdom, dark paths lure.

Streams murmur secrets to the night,
Reflecting the silver of moonlight bright,
Silent wishes in their flow light,
In nature's symphony, hearts unite.

Mountains stand guard in stoic grace,
Embracing the world in a cold embrace,
Their peaks touch the celestial space,
Silent witnesses of time's trace.

Stars woven in the cosmic thread,
Guide dreams where angels gently tread,
In this realm where silence has bled,
Hollows of harmony, peace spread.

Underneath It All

Beneath the layers, truths reside,
In shadows where our fears abide.
Whispers echo through the hall,
Secrets lie, underneath it all.

Mysteries wrapped in dark embrace,
Veiled in the folds of time and space.
Unknown forces rise and fall,
Whispers heard, underneath it all.

Beneath the surface, stillness reigns,
Silent tides and hidden chains.
Life concealed, reflections small,
Journeys made, underneath it all.

Subterranean Whispers

In the depths, where shadows play,
Whispers guide the cautious way.
Through the tunnels, long and tall,
Secret voices softly call.

Ancient words in caverns deep,
Guard the secrets that they keep.
Echoes from the earthen hall,
Silent tales the walls recall.

Below the earth, a hidden song,
Carried on the winds so strong.
Subterranean whispers fall,
Tales untold, heard by all.

The Hidden Pathways

Among the roots, the pathways lie,
Winding where few dare to try.
Beneath the soil, trails unseen,
Hidden paths that intervene.

Footprints lost in soft embrace,
Leading to a secret place.
Through the dark and winding ways,
Silent guides through hidden days.

Lightless roads in silent night,
Paths that lead beyond the sight.
Through the earth, where secrets stay,
Hidden pathways show the way.

Caverns of Silence

Silent caverns bound in stone,
Echoes of a world unknown.
Stillness in each hollowed hall,
Silent whispers, standing tall.

Within the dark, where light has fled,
Shadows weave where fears are bred.
Caverns deep and whispers small,
Silent voices call and call.

In the quiet, peace unfolds,
Tales of old the silence holds.
Caverns of a world concealed,
Silent secrets are revealed.

Earth's Embrace

Beneath the sky's azure quilt,
Fields of green in silence tilt,
Mountains rise, a timeless grace,
Nature's arms, an endless place.

Whispers of the ancient trees,
Dancing leaves in autumn's breeze,
Rivers carve their winding course,
Life renews its endless source.

Morning's dew on petals bright,
Softly kissed by dawn's first light,
Creatures roam in rightful space,
In Earth's gentle, warm embrace.

Hidden Masterpieces

Museums carved in hidden stone,
Histories in whispers known,
Layers deep, like secret scrolls,
Art of old, with ancient souls.

In shadows, sculpted minds reside,
Tales and truths they never hide,
Brushes woven in the dark,
Painting dreams with timeless spark.

Voices of forgotten time,
Silenced yet forever prime,
Masterpieces left unseen,
Shadows that have always been.

Veiled Ventures

Journeys cloaked in twilight's shade,
Paths where light and dark cascade,
Steps unknown, in realms unseen,
Ventures shadowed, yet so keen.

Stars imprisoned by the night,
Guiding whispers out of sight,
Mysteries around each turn,
In the dark, new fires burn.

Secrets held in silence deep,
Wonders waking from their sleep,
Every shadow hides a tale,
Veiled ventures never pale.

Glimpses Below

Beneath the surface, hidden sights,
Creatures move in silent nights,
Worlds below, where few will go,
Deep within, they ebb and flow.

Caverns hum with ancient song,
Echoes whisper, clear and strong,
Treasures buried far from light,
Secrets kept in endless night.

Depths where stories softly glow,
Mysteries only shadows know,
Life beneath, in ebb and flow,
Glimpses seen from far below.

Soft Shelters

In whispers, leaves do nestle tight,
Under moon's elusive light.
Homes crafted in the evening's breath,
Guarded by night's silent depth.

A fold of moss, a cove concealed,
Secrets in twilight revealed.
Where dreams find space to weave and roam,
Soft shelters call this refuge home.

Shadows craft a gentle weave,
As night begins its subtle heave.
Cradled by the wind's embrace,
Peace finds us in this quiet place.

Depth's Dance

In ocean depths, where secrets glide,
Tales of old beneath the tide.
Fishes sway with fins so free,
In a dance of mystery.

Corals blaze in colors bright,
Dawn and dusk intertwined light.
Every move a rhythmic grace,
Depth's dance in a boundless space.

Whales' songs whisper through the deep,
In melodies our hearts they keep.
Down below where silence roars,
Depth's dance opens unseen doors.

Violin of the Void

Strings of stars strum cosmic tunes,
Midnight symphony under moons.
Galaxies hum in silent glee,
Violin of the void, set free.

Nebulae like velvet bow,
Sweeping through the space's flow.
Each note, a twinkle in the night,
Melodies of distant light.

Planets spin in rhythmic trance,
Orbiting in timeless dance.
In the void, a song unspoiled,
Played on a violin uncoiled.

Carved by Claws

Mountains etched in dawn's first light,
Silent sentinels of the night.
Carved by claws of time and storm,
Nature's art in rawest form.

Winds that bear a savage grace,
Shape the earth in fierce embrace.
Each canyon and each jagged scar,
Tells tales of where ancient claws are.

Rivers etched in timeless play,
Charting paths from night to day.
Carved by claws of nature wild,
Earth's own story reconciled.

Hidden Passageway

In forests dense, where shadows play,
A hidden path, long lost to day,
Beneath the boughs, it twists and winds,
A secret tale in nature's lines.

Soft mossy steps where fairies tread,
Whispers of dreams, by green leaves fed,
This ancient trail, forgotten now,
Holds mysteries beneath each bough.

A door of bark, a latch unseen,
To realms where only stars have been,
This wayward path, through time it weaves,
In sylvan hearts, old magic breathes.

Beyond the oak, the way grows clear,
A portal where the brave draw near,
To seek the past in twilight's crest,
And find the lore where shadows rest.

Veins of the Earth

Through stony veins, the lifeblood flows,
Beneath our feet, where darkness grows,
The earth's own pulse, in caverns deep,
Where ancient secrets lie and sleep.

Rivers cold with whispers old,
Fossil tales that time has told,
Echoes long from ages past,
In earthen hearts their spells are cast.

Roots like fingers, reaching low,
Into the dark where secrets sow,
Binding earth in silent grace,
Connecting all in hidden space.

Veins of gold and iron thread,
Silent songs of what lies ahead,
Within the earth's embrace we find,
A story writ in stone and mind.

Nature's Quiet Architects

Beneath the leaves, they hidden weave,
The silent art they interleave,
Small creatures craft their master plan,
The architects unseen by man.

The spider's silk, a silver thread,
A web of dreams in nature spread,
With patience rare, they spin the night,
Creating form from sheer delight.

Ants below in trails so thin,
Carving paths where life begins,
They build their homes with earth and toil,
A network vast beneath the soil.

Bees construct with waxen skill,
Their hives with honeycombed will,
From tiny acts, a world is spun,
By nature's hand, the work is done.

Secret Tunnels

Beneath our feet, the night descends,
Where secret tunnels twist and bend,
A maze of clay and silent dark,
Holds whispered tales and hidden spark.

Through earthy walls, the burrows wind,
With every turn, a world confined,
The unseen paths where creatures roam,
In shadowed halls, they find their home.

Below the ground, in twilight's keep,
The roots of trees like serpents creep,
They bridge the gaps and anchor deep,
While life above in silence sleeps.

In secret tunnels, stories flow,
Of ancient force we rarely know,
A world beneath that breathes and lives,
In realms of dirt, its wisdom gives.

Treasure Beneath

Beneath the earth, where shadows play,
Hidden gems in quiet stay.
In caverns deep and mines so old,
Lies treasure more than glittering gold.

Through darkness thick and silence wide,
Secrets of time in stone do hide.
With careful foot and watchful eye,
Seekers venture, not knowing why.

Songs of minerals, tales of ore,
Echo softly, forevermore.
Chisel bites and lanterns gleam,
Shards of history through the seam.

Ancient whispers, soil-infused,
Oceans past, by time amused.
Crystals dance with muted glow,
Nature's art from depths below.

The quest goes on, no end in sight,
Digging dreams both day and night.
For in the earth, where shadows breathe,
Lies the world, our treasure beneath.

Digging Dreams

In the realm where night does split,
Miners delve, their lanterns lit.
Every strike upon the rock,
Awakens dreams in earth's own clock.

With pick in hand and heart's desire,
They chase the gold in earthen fire.
Faith and hope their guiding beams,
In the quest of life's own dreams.

Echoes of the past they greet,
Marks of old beneath their feet.
Sepia tones and ghostly wings,
Brush their skin as silence sings.

Visions vivid, through the strife,
Of brighter days and fuller life.
In shadows cast by mountain seams,
They find the spark in digging dreams.

Through the nights of toil and sweat,
They seek the treasures not yet met.
For dreams are born in darkest scenes,
Down the path of digging dreams.

Chambers of Solitude

In chambers deep where silence reigns,
Solitude unravels chains.
Each breath echoes through the dark,
In solitude, they leave their mark.

The walls remember, ages past,
Voices gone, yet echoes last.
Hollow spaces, empty frames,
Hold the weight of countless names.

A solitary lantern's glow,
Reveals the path where brave hearts go.
In the stillness, burdens fade,
Strength drawn from the quiet shade.

Ancient whispers softly tread,
In the quiet, truths are said.
Within these walls, one's soul renews,
In solitude, new pathways choose.

In chambers vast, where silence soothes,
Life's complexities subtly lose.
For deep within the earth's vast brood,
Lie the secrets of solitude.

Subterranean Whispers

Beneath the world's fast turning spree,
Lie whispers of the earth's decree.
In tunnels carved by time and hand,
Subterranean voices stand.

They speak of roots and ancient coils,
Of bygone days and buried toils.
In every crevice, every fold,
Are tales of quiet, still untold.

Small echoes drift on breezes thin,
Of creatures past and places dim.
They paint the walls in palimpsest,
Stories yearning for their rest.

In labyrinths, where silence speaks,
Answers found that wisdom seeks.
A gentle hum, a soft refrain,
Carried through each stony vein.

Subterranean whispers flow,
In hidden caves where secrets grow.
In dark and dusk, life's softest hymns,
Are sung in stone by nature's whims.

Beneath

Underneath the seamless sky,
In the hush where shadows lie,
Dreams do flutter, softly sigh,
Hidden worlds are nigh.

Far from light's revealing flare,
Secrets whisper, souls laid bare,
Roots entwine in earthy care,
Mystery strips the air.

Whither stands the veiled abyss,
Soft embraced by night's sweet kiss,
Questions rise in moonlit mist,
Bound by what we miss.

Beneath the surface, life's array,
Boundless journeys, night and day,
Nature's quiet, silent sway,
In the dark, we lay.

Beyond

Stars aligned in distant froth,
Unseen waves, the cosmic broth,
Travelers sail, minds aloft,
Seeking what they sought.

Past the veils of time and space,
Eyes ascend, embrace the chase,
Truths unfurled in glowing lace,
Hope in cosmic face.

Galaxies in endless spin,
Secrets held in nebula spin,
Vistas wide and dreams within,
Whence the quest begin.

Beyond the known, the future lies,
Wisdom sage in ether's ties,
As we venture to the skies,
Ever to belies.

The Resilient Tunneler

Through the soil, steadfast bore,
Silent whispers, nature's lore,
As the tunnels slowly pore,
Life beneath the floor.

Persistent path, none can see,
By the roots and darkened tree,
Carving earth most valiantly,
In the shadows free.

Against the odds, they forge ahead,
Beneath the surface where dreams are spread,
Crafting homes from ground and dread,
In dark quarries led.

Resilient heart, unyielding core,
Silent strength, forevermore,
In the earthbound worlds they soar,
To create and explore.

The Clover's Companion

Beside the clover in the field,
Where thoughts in gentle breezes yield,
Companions close, in bonds are sealed,
Nature's joy revealed.

Whispers of the morning dew,
Petals bright in verdant hue,
In the quiet, life renew,
With each day anew.

Tales of seasons passed in cheer,
Through the lapsing of the year,
Together standing strong and clear,
In the meadows near.

As the world in time does spin,
Kindred spirits gather in,
Clover's grace on nature's whim,
With the spring to begin.

Earth’s Silent Sculptor

Hidden depths where shadows play,
Take form in gradual, gentle sway,
Sculpting lives in secret ways,
Earth’s grand essay.

Careful hands of time unseen,
Shape the mountains, valleys green,
In patience, whispers intervene,
Nature’s chiseled scene.

With quiet grace, they mold and tear,
Creatures great and small they spare,
Endless touch in silence' care,
In the crafted air.

Forms arise from stealthy touch,
Miracles in earth's soft clutch,
Silent moves that yield so much,
In life's endless crutch.

Silent Sculptors

In twilight's gentle hands, they carve
What shadows whisper in the dark,
Silent sculptors, hearts so starved,
For beauty, their eternal mark.

Through marble veins and granite dreams,
They chisel truths that often weep,
In whispers heard but never seen,
Their secrets buried cold and deep.

With every stroke, a story sings,
Of ancient love and bitter wars,
The hammer's echo softly rings,
Embodying forgotten lore.

In silent halls where echoes fade,
Their work endures, a timeless hush,
As night and day in balance swayed,
Their art commands a gentle hush.

In twilight's grasp, their spirits glow,
Silent sculptors, hearts laid bare,
Through every shape, their essence shows,
A legacy of tender care.

Corners of the Undergrowth

In corners of the undergrowth,
Where shadows dance and secrets lie,
The whispers of the forest cloak,
The tales of those who've slipped nearby.

Through tangled vines and mossy stones,
A pathway veiled in twilight's gleam,
The air, a mix of whispered moans,
And echoes of a distant dream.

With rustling leaves and creaking boughs,
The forest breathes a living song,
In hidden nooks, the watcher prowls,
Where day and night unite the throng.

The creatures know these sacred paths,
Their silent steps won't break the spell,
In corners of the undergrowth,
They weave their tales and bid farewell.

For here, beneath the canopy,
Where sunlight filters through the haze,
The secrets of the world unfold,
In nature's quiet, endless maze.

Navigating Nests

Within the branches stretched toward sky,
They weave a hope, a fragile thread,
Navigating nests awry,
Where life and love together spread.

Through wind and storm, they build anew,
Their refuge, cradles made with care,
Each twig a promise, strong and true,
A haven high in open air.

Their flight a dance of pure intent,
With wings that brush the heavens' face,
Navigating nests they've dreamt,
In endless search for safety's grace.

At dawn's embrace and evening's hush,
They nurture young with tender beak,
In borrowed time, amid the rush,
Their wisdom unfolds, silent, meek.

Within the branches, tales are told,
Of journeys, heartache, joy, and rest,
Navigating nests of gold,
Where life's brave heartbeat finds its nest.

Rain's Refuge

Beneath the storm's relentless kiss,
A refuge found in rain's embrace,
The world, a symphony of bliss,
In every drop, a soft trace.

Sheltered under heaven's sighs,
We watch the skies release their tears,
A dance of sorrow, sweet goodbyes,
That washes away hidden fears.

The earth absorbs each tender fall,
Reviving thirst with gentle touch,
While nature's voice begins to call,
In rain's refuge, we find so much.

In whispered pitter-patter songs,
The rhythm lulls our troubled mind,
Where sorrow's weight no longer throngs,
And peace within the storm we find.

Beneath the storm's relentless kiss,
A haven formed of liquid grace,
Rain's refuge grants a quiet bliss,
Where hearts find solace in its trace.

Soil's Embrace

Beneath the waltzing leaves, we lie,
In earthen beds, where secrets sigh.
Roots weave stories, old and deep,
In soil's embrace, we gently sleep.

Muffled hum of nature's heart,
From life below, we cannot part.
The loam and clay, our shelter vast,
A silent echo of the past.

In darkened depths, the world anew,
With every drop of morning dew.
Whispers of the ancient rain,
To nourish, heal, and end our pain.

In fertile dark, we find our peace,
As seasons turn, and dreams release.
Among the roots, through time's expanse,
In soil's embrace, life's fervent dance.

Deep Dwelling Days

Within the ground, the stories hide,
Where shadows shift and memories bide.
The quiet hum of days gone by,
In deep dwelling, we learn to sigh.

The whispering of ancient trees,
Soft murmurs carried by the breeze.
In hollows dark, our secrets keep,
Among the roots, our sorrows weep.

The earth beneath, a tender grave,
For dreams elusive, bold, and brave.
We linger where the roots entwine,
In quietude, our souls align.

Each layer tells a tale untold,
Of times and lives in soil enfold.
In deep dwelling days, serene,
We find the peace in what has been.

Hushed Enclaves

Within the hushed enclaves of night,
Where shadows dance in faint moonlight.
We find a peace, both soft and rare,
In whispers carried on the air.

Among the trees, the world stands still,
A silent breath, a gentle thrill.
The stars above in silence gleam,
In hushed enclaves, we drift and dream.

No upheaval, no loud refrain,
Just pulsing life in pure sustain.
The whispers of the leaves we heed,
In tender quiet, we take our lead.

The peace we find in silent bowers,
In hidden glades and quiet hours.
In hushed enclaves, the world seems right,
A lullaby of soft twilight.

Cradled by Clods

In the cradling clods, our heart does rest,
In earthen arms, we are truly blessed.
The soil's embrace, a tender fold,
Where dreams of yore are quietly told.

The warmth of earth, a soft cocoon,
Beneath the rays of dappled moon.
In nature's grip, so firm and kind,
We leave our worldly woes behind.

In clods that bear the weight of life,
Connected hearts, devoid of strife.
The scent of grass, of blooming seed,
In fertile ground, we plant our creed.

The cradle of clods, a timeless song,
Where every soul can feel they belong.
In this embrace, so wide, profound,
We find the peace, the love unbound.

Digging Through Time

In earth's embrace, the past sleeps sound,
Layers of secrets, all around.
Digging deep, through years we tread,
Unveil the tales, the earth has bled.

Eons whisper from the ground,
Chronicles in silence found.
Time-locked stories, cold and deep,
Through shattered bones, the ages seep.

From ancient sun and moon so bright,
To shadows born of endless night.
History hums in buried tune,
Beneath our feet, a time cocoon.

Each turn of soil brings forth a name,
An echo of some long-lost flame.
Memories trapped in stone and clay,
Revealing worlds from yesterday.

A spade, a brush, a quest so grand,
To touch the past with gentle hand.
For in this earth, where ages blend,
We find the echoes of the end.

Beneath the Surface

Beneath the surface, worlds unseen,
A hidden realm of blue and green.
In silence, life begins to weave,
The stories that the waters leave.

The tendrils of the seaweed sway,
In whispers of a soft ballet.
The currents sing their ancient song,
Where secret lives and shadows throng.

Through caverns dark and reefs so bright,
Creatures dance in moon's soft light.
Their secrets held in ocean's breath,
A living world where life and death.

From deepest trench to tidal crest,
The underwater heart's unrest.
Whispers of an ancient tide,
In waves of time, the moments bide.

The surface glows with morning's grace,
Yet hidden depths we long to trace.
For in the ocean's gentle flow,
A silent world that yearns to show.

The Burrower's Tale

Deep within the earthen bed,
Where many fears and dreams have fled.
Lies the path the burrower knows,
A labyrinth where silence grows.

Through roots and stones, the journey wends,
In darkness where the day descends.
A whisper soft of earth's embrace,
A hidden, peaceful, guarded place.

Each tunnel leads to stories new,
Of buried secrets, none but few.
The soil retains what once was lost,
Beneath the frost where time is tossed.

In solitude, the burrow thrives,
In quietude where life derives.
A scholar of the darkened depths,
Through sunless halls, the spirit kept.

A kingdom small yet infinite,
The burrower holds counsel with.
For in the earth, we find the way,
A silent tale of night and day.

Veins of the Earth

Veins of the earth, in silent weave,
A hidden lore they yet conceive.
Far beneath footsteps above,
Flows the life, the earth's own love.

In caverns dark and fissures grand,
The secrets of this ancient land.
Echoes of a breathless age,
Written in a stony page.

Rivers run where light shall fade,
In the stillness they are made.
From molten core to frozen crest,
The earth in constant, quiet quest.

Veins that pulse with nature's might,
From morning's dawn to deepest night.
Carry forward the earth's own song,
In rhythms true where they belong.

Beneath the ground we stand upon,
The hidden streams of time have gone.
In every pulse, a silent call,
The earth's own heart beats through it all.

Buried Horizons

The sun set deep beneath the fields,
Horizon hidden 'neath plow's yield.
In earth's embrace, a story sealed,
Unseen realms are now revealed.

Gold and amber light once shown,
Now subdued in twilight's tone.
Seeds of dreams in furrows sown,
Buried visions, never known.

Ancient whispers, fields enclose,
Mystic tales in soil, compose.
Eternal cycle, life bestows,
Hidden paths that nature chose.

Silent echoes, time has claimed,
Roots of yore, by earth unnamed.
Horizons buried, yet untamed,
In dusk's embrace, they're framed.

Through the furrows, shadows creep,
Secrets in the darkness sleep.
In the earth, our memories keep,
Horizon's guardians, buried deep.

Whispered Caverns

In caverns deep, where echoes play,
Where whispered winds through shadows sway.
Myst'ry in each turn and bay,
Secrets old, beneath the day.

Crystal tears from stalactite,
Songs of silence, pure and bright.
Hidden worlds, devoid of light,
Whispered tales by moonless night.

Rocky walls, with life in trace,
Ancient whispers fill the space.
Nature's hand, in slow embrace,
Crafts the cavern's stony face.

Rivers murmuring through the dark,
Softly singing, leaves a mark.
In depths where dreams may spark,
Whispered thoughts, like Noah's ark.

Echoes linger, voices blend,
Veils of darkness never end.
To the caverns' depths, descend,
Whispered secrets, time will send.

Nestled by Soil

In the cradle of soil, dreams reside,
Nestled close, beneath the tide.
Life's essence, in earth applied,
Nature's spirits, far and wide.

Roots entwine in darkened cover,
In the earth, they twist and hover.
Life in slumber, yet discover,
Lessons whispered by a lover.

Seeds and stories interlace,
In each layer, time and space.
Earth's arms, a warm embrace,
Holding close, the past's trace.

Beneath the surface, wonders stay,
Hidden gems in brown and gray.
Silent tales in form of clay,
Nature's guardians, night and day.

Through the soil, life's pulse sustained,
Wisdom in each grain contained.
Nestled close, like the unchained,
By the soil, where dreams are gained.

Earth's Hidden Quilt

Beneath the surface, colors weave,
A hidden quilt we can't perceive.
Life’s mysteries, in patterns leave,
Secrets that the earth does cleave.

Vibrant threads in quiet scape,
Nature’s art in each escape.
Tales of soil, in forms reshape,
Life interwoven, no escape.

Depths where shadows softly weave,
Ancient secrets they conceive.
In the loam, past lives perceive,
Earth's hidden quilt, they achieve.

Layer by layer, textures blend,
In the soil, no start, no end.
Earth’s embrace, like a friend,
In each fiber, wisdom penned.

Quilt of wonders, stitched by time,
In the earth, a silent chime.
Whispers of a world sublime,
Hidden beauty, so divine.

Buried Harmony

In the earth where secrets keep,
Dreams lie dormant, fast asleep,
Roots entwine in whispered song,
Silent echoes, ages long.

Nature's hymn beneath the ground,
Symphonies in silence found,
Rustling leaves a muted choir,
Fading echoes, dark and dire.

Crickets chirp in twilight's grace,
Moonlight bathes the hidden place,
Whispers of the ancient night,
Buried harmony in sight.

Nooks of Night

In shadowed corners, midnight falls,
Stars ignite in cosmic halls,
Silence speaks in softest breath,
Night encloses, hides from death.

Mystic realms in dark embrace,
Time stands still in ebon grace,
Owl's hoot echoes through the air,
Secrets deep within its stare.

Lantern light on cobblestone,
Guides the way when night is grown,
Mysteries in every flight,
Woven in the nooks of night.

Ancient Pathways

Steps forgotten, moss has laid,
On trails where time begins to fade,
Cobblestones of stories old,
Whispers of a journey bold.

Fallen arches, ivy's grasp,
Tales of yore in nature's clasp,
Branches sway with hints of past,
Breathing life in shadows cast.

Heed the call of ancient ways,
Footfalls mark the passing days,
Elders' ghosts in twilight roam,
Ancient pathways lead them home.

Gentle Descent

Leaves cascade in autumn's breath,
Silent hymn to summer's death,
Colors blend in twilight hues,
Nature whispers soft adieus.

River flows in graceful bends,
To the sea where journey ends,
Mountains peak and valleys sigh,
Underneath a pastel sky.

Downward flight of evening birds,
Murmured lull in softened words,
Settle softly, close the day,
Gentle descent fades away.

Underground Galleries

Beneath the earth, where secrets sigh,
In vaults that twine and turn,
The hidden tales of time gone by,
In darkness softly burn.

A painter's brush in shadowed hands,
Etched whispers fill the air,
Art unfurls 'neath unseen lands,
In crypts without a care.

Underfoot, an artful maze,
Halls of stone and echo,
Winding through the timeless haze,
Where only shadows go.

Colors bloom without the light,
Shapes that twist and tremble,
In the womb of endless night,
Mysteries assemble.

Stalagmites like candles glow,
In chambers deep and hollow,
Silent tales of long ago,
Where only brave souls follow.

Sheltered by Shadows

In the valley, where shadows dwell,
Beneath a twilight sky,
Quiet whispers weave their spell,
As moonlit winds drift by.

A sanctuary of the dusk,
Cloaks the world in gray,
Where the air is cool and musk,
The light begins to sway.

Walls of shadow, roof of night,
A refuge soft and still,
A gentle dance of dark and light,
That weaves its cherished thrill.

In secret boughs, dark secrets keep,
A shelter from the sun,
In nighttime's arms, the world asleep,
We find our rest begun.

Lost in shadows, we are free,
From the glaring day,
Sheltered by the night's decree,
In shadows, safe, we stay.

Whispered Thoroughfares

Along the paths where whispers tread,
Soft voices call and beckon,
Where silent secrets lie ahead,
In every hidden beckon.

Cobblestones of whispered dreams,
Pave the quiet lanes,
Each footfall softer than it seems,
Where mystery remains.

Through corridors by shadows kissed,
We walk in hushed delight,
In labyrinths by twilight dressed,
That hide us from the light.

Each alleyway a whispered prayer,
A tale that's softly spun,
In muted tones that fill the air,
Where quiet stories run.

As twilight falls and shadows play,
These paths of gentle sound,
Lead us to where the whispers stay,
In secrecy profound.

Delicate Excavations

With careful hand, the earth revealed,
Secrets long concealed,
In whispers of the ancient field,
Histories are healed.

Each gentle brush a story wakes,
From silence deep and long,
In layers where the earth partakes,
A whispered, buried song.

Artifacts of life once bright,
Now shadows of the past,
Delicate in dawn’s first light,
Revealing truths that last.

Fragments of a time gone by,
Beneath the soil’s embrace,
Resurrected breath and sigh,
From their hidden place.

In the quiet dig, a slow unveil,
Of lives that came before,
Delicate as a whispered tale,
We unearth forgotten lore.

Secrets from Underground

In the quiet earth, deep below,
Whispers of secrets softly show,
Hidden chambers, dark and vast,
Echoes of a forgotten past.

Motes of dust, in still air dance,
Guardians of a silent trance,
Ancient bones, in stories blend,
Where the shadows never end.

Silent rivers, cold and deep,
Hold the dreams that never sleep,
Caverns stretch, in twilight’s fold,
Tales of treasures, yet untold.

Veins of ore, and seams of clay,
Mark the path where legends lay,
Mysteries in darkness bloom,
Untouched by the sun's bright plume.

Down where daylight fears to tread,
Voices from the ages wed,
In the secret depths below,
Whispers from the past still flow.

Nature's Hidden Craft

In the forest's hidden core,
Crafted secrets, ancient lore,
Roots entwined in earthen grace,
Life's deep artistry in place.

Leaves and branches intertwine,
Silent songs in subtle line,
Nature crafts with unseen hands,
Masterpieces in the sands.

Tiny creatures, skilled and bright,
Build their homes out of sight,
Each a master, in the mold,
Of the stories that unfold.

Morning dew, on spider's lace,
Catches light, in strong embrace,
Glittering threads, by night unfurled,
Weaving wonders in the world.

Gardens rise in shaded glen,
Crafted far from eyes of men,
Nature's hand, with gentle art,
Shapes the world in every part.

The Quiet Digger

In the stillness, there he toils,
Quiet in the darkened soils,
With each turn, the earth he bends,
Finding where the silence ends.

Gentle hands, with care and grace,
Move the earth in light embrace,
In the shadows, close and near,
Silent stories he will hear.

Burrows deep, a world unseen,
Where the timeless roots convene,
Every clump and clod explored,
In the silence, secrets stored.

Listening to the heartbeat slow,
Of the earth and what it knows,
In each layer, truth will gleam,
Underneath the daylight's beam.

The quiet digger, with his craft,
Shifts the earth, so slow, so daft,
Finding what the world conceals,
In the silence, life reveals.

Beneath the Roots

Beneath the roots, a world lies still,
Hidden deep where sun can't spill,
Labyrinth of winding veins,
Holds the secrets where life remains.

Silent whispers, tales untold,
Twisted through the loam and mold,
Ancient hands, in shadows mark,
Life's own pulse in regions dark.

Roots embrace the soil tight,
Guardians of earthbound night,
In their arms, the secrets keep,
Memories in shadows sleep.

In the depths, where few can see,
Lies the earth's own mystery,
Beneath the roots, the silence hums,
Where creation's echo drums.

Deep within the earth's own core,
Sunless seas and whispered lore,
Legacy of time holds fast,
In the roots, the truth is cast.

Darkened Labyrinths

Amidst the shadows, cold and still,
Where moonlight dares not trace.
Whispers echo from the walls,
In this forsaken place.

Steps unsure on ancient stones,
Specters of the past collide.
Lost within the twisted maze,
My soul, I can’t confide.

Torches flicker, guiding weak,
Winds howl a chilling song.
In these darkened labyrinths,
The nights stretch ever-long.

Hope flickers, faint but true,
A beacon in the black.
Through the winding corridors,
There’s no turning back.

Labyrinths of fate and fear,
Holding secrets, old and vast.
Braving through the shadows thick,
I find my peace at last.

Secret Soil Streets

Hidden pathways green and gold,
Beneath the forest's veil.
Ancient roots and tangled vines,
Whisper secret tales.

The sky a canopy of dreams,
Leaves rustle soft and sweet.
Mysteries of earth and lore,
In secret soil streets.

Steps in silence, heart in tune,
Nature's sacred dance.
Colors paint a vibrant song,
In this quiet trance.

Sunbeams play through branches high,
A symphony of light.
Guiding wanderers to peace,
In the day and night.

These secret streets of earth and wonder,
Hold stories to unfold.
In the heart of nature's silence,
A thousand dreams are told.

Voices in the Deep

Echoes roll in caverns vast,
Where sunlight never beams.
A symphony of whispered words,
From distant, unknown dreams.

Walls adorned with ancient marks,
Stories etched in stone.
Voices in the deep resound,
Where souls are left alone.

Depths conceal the mysteries,
Of time's immortal keep.
Shadows cast their endless night,
In silence, secrets sleep.

Cold embrace of darkened realms,
A haven for the lost.
Among the voices in the deep,
Their burdens, whispers cost.

Yet in the depth, a guiding light,
A voice that leads astray.
To find within the endless dark,
A new and hopeful day.

Burrowed Paths

Through the earth, a hidden trail,
Where secrets softly breeze.
Roots embrace the ancient way,
In whispers, nature's ease.

Burrowed paths through time and soil,
Carry tales untold.
Every step a journey vast,
In whispers, life unfolds.

Underneath the canopy,
Where shadows softly play.
Burrowed paths of silence lead,
To light of breaking day.

Earthbound dreams await the tread,
Of wanderers who seek.
In the quiet of the earth,
Voices old and meek.

Burrow deep and find the calm,
Of nature’s hidden psalm.
Walk the paths of earth and thought,
In serenity and calm.

Soil's Silent Songs

Beneath the crust, where roots entwine,
A hidden life begins to shine.
Whispers of earth, so deep, so vast,
Tell of a future and a past.

Worms weave tales in hidden nooks,
In soil’s embrace, the old, the new looks.
Silent melodies, earth’s sweet refrain,
Songs of life, of loss, of gain.

A pebble’s journey from mount to mire,
A song that's sung by nature’s choir.
Each clump of soil, a verse to spare,
In nature’s book, so pure, so rare.

Decayed leaves become life anew,
In darkness deep where spirits flew.
In silence, soil’s soft secrets throng,
A symphony, sweet soil’s song.

Stillness above, below life's hue,
A world unseen, yet ever true.
In quiet depths, life's song prolongs,
Eternal are soil's silent songs.

The Quiet Excavation

Shovels part the earth with care,
Revealing treasures hidden there.
Layers peeled, and stories told,
Of lands unseen, both new and old.

Minerals gleam in soft deceit,
In graves of silence, in dark retreat.
Digging whispers, secrets past,
In quiet breaths, their spell is cast.

Artifacts of ages found,
In depths where time and earth are bound.
Each stroke of spade, a silent quest,
In soil’s deep vault, we find our rest.

Echoes of a world bygone,
In whispered winds, in early dawn.
The soil gives voice to history,
In every grain, a mystery.

Unseen realms with life abate,
In quiet excavation, fate.
Delving deep in earth’s embrace,
We unearth time, we find our place.

Beneath the Layers

Beneath the grass, beneath the dew,
A world unseen, both old and new.
Layers deep, where shadows blend,
In silent whispers, stories mend.

Pebbles mark the pathways gone,
Roots connect the dusk to dawn.
In every layer, life's refrain,
Cycles bound in endless chain.

Fossils of dreams in compact wait,
Buried in the sands of fate.
Traces of a life once lived,
In earth's embrace, all dreams forgave.

Ancient secrets softly lie,
Beneath the soil, the earth, the sky.
In layers rich, in hues profound,
The essence of life's cycle found.

Volcano's ash and river silt,
Stories of the lands we built.
In every stratum, time replays,
The silent truths, beneath the layers.

Digging in Silence

With spade in hand, the earth we breach,
In silence, where few dare to reach.
Each stroke a pause, a quiet thought,
In soil's embrace, truth is sought.

Roots entwine in secret bands,
Silent stewards of the lands.
Digging deep, the echoes yield,
Lessons from nature, quietly revealed.

In caverns dark, where shadows stay,
Life persists in its own way.
The silent dig, a quest untold,
In earth’s womb, the secrets hold.

Scattered bones of ancient form,
Silent whispers, past storms.
In silence, earth’s history,
Revealed through quiet mystery.

Beneath the murmur of the sky,
Silent tombs in layers lie.
Deep we dig, in mindful trance,
In silence, earth’s reticence.

Through the Wormhole

Stars align, twisting space and time,
Galaxies dance in a cosmic rhyme,
Journey begun, to realms unknown,
Through wormholes, our fate is shown.

Light bends as we sail through the dark,
Time collapses, a cosmic spark,
Parallel worlds in a twinkling blur,
Mysteries unfold, destinies stir.

Voyage beyond the mortal sphere,
Echoes of existence both far and near,
Gravity’s grip begins to wane,
Boundaries dissolve, merging plane.

Whispers of a vanished race,
Traces of hope left in empty space,
Through the wormholes, wisdom gleams,
Future unfolds in stellar dreams.

Returning home, new stars we chart,
Ephemeral dreams leave an eternal mark,
Infinite realms in the time we borrowed,
Through the wormholes, futures are harrowed.

Subterranean Secrets

Beneath the earth where shadows dance,
Lies a world of hidden chance,
Crystals gleam in the silent cave,
Legends whisper, secrets brave.

Roots entwine in the ancient deep,
Guarding tales that shadows keep,
Murmurs rise from the soil's breath,
Echoes of life beyond death.

Under layers of stone and clay,
Undisturbed by the light of day,
Treasures buried, unseen, unknown,
Subterranean secrets overgrown.

Caverns echo with silent songs,
Mysteries of where life belongs,
Veins of ore, stories old and new,
Lode of Earth's tales, hidden from view.

Explorers seek the enigmatic hue,
Through tunnels winding, they pursue,
Subterranean chambers, ageless and wide,
Secrets of Earth eternally hide.

Layers of Life

Peeling back layers of history's page,
Lives entwined in an endless stage,
A human tapestry, rich and bright,
Stories of sorrow turned to light.

Generations pass like whispers in wind,
Each layer with lessons twinned,
From birth to death, a cyclical dance,
Life's perpetual, fleeting chance.

Patterns emerge from years long gone,
Echoes of triumphs linger on,
In every layer, a tale untold,
Rich with wisdom, bright and bold.

Untangling threads of times ahead,
Colors blend, though paths have fled,
In each fragment, life’s melody,
Layers of joy and agony.

Deep within the strata of soul,
The essence of existence is whole,
Layers of life, woven and spun,
In unity, we are all one.

Deeply Hidden

In the quiet, deeply hidden realm,
Where shadows sway and night overwhelm,
Secrets whisper in the dark's embrace,
Mysteries linger, leaving no trace.

Veiled truths beneath the silent stream,
Locked within a midnight dream,
Ancient woods conceal with grace,
Deeply hidden in nature’s place.

Mountain’s heart where light is rare,
Caves of secrets, layered with care,
Whispers of winds through hollowed stone,
Deeply hidden but not alone.

Beneath the ocean’s vast abyss,
Lies a world of hidden bliss,
Creatures thrive in realms unseen,
Ephemeral glow in turquoise sheen.

In each heart, a hidden space,
Guarding truths with gentle embrace,
Deeply hidden, where souls unite,
In twilight's gentle, quiet light.

Stories From Below

In shadows deep where secrets lie,
The tales of old come creeping by.
Roots and stones, their whispers tell,
Of ancient times beneath the swell.

Worms that weave through earth’s embrace,
Crafting paths in unseen grace.
Mysteries hidden, buried deep,
In soil's quiet, secrets sleep.

Bones of beasts and seeds of kin,
Hold the past in silence thin.
Layered epochs, strata's tale,
Underneath, life's hidden veil.

Minerals gleam in darkness bright,
Gems that capture lost moonlight.
Fossils speak of life once known,
Earth's own memory, set in stone.

Listen close, for in the ground,
Stories from below resound.
Timeless echoes, whispers low,
History's roots, where life does grow.

Beneath the Woodland

Underneath the forest floor,
Lies a world of endless lore.
Roots entwine in secret dance,
Nature’s own romance, entrance.

Mushrooms bloom like fairy lights,
Glow amidst the darkened nights.
Mossy carpets, soft and green,
Blanket realms that stay unseen.

Critters carve their hidden homes,
Beneath the trees, where no one roams.
Beetles, ants in endless quest,
Building lives in earthen nest.

Nutrients cycle, life's own thread,
Keeping green the canopy's spread.
Silent keepers of the trees,
Toiling where no sunlight sees.

Whispering winds through roots below,
Carry stories old and slow.
Beneath the woodland, life aligns,
In harmony, the forest signs.

Soil’s Silent Workers

In depths where sunlight does not tread,
Titanic toils remain unsaid.
Worms and beetles work the ground,
Life's foundation, so profound.

Turning earth with tireless might,
From dark to dark, both day and night.
Fertile soil by humble hand,
Forms the base on which we stand.

Microbes teem in hidden streams,
Crafting health by unseen means.
Nurturing the roots that rise,
To touch the world beneath the skies.

Decaying leaves and fallen wood,
Recycled, turned to nature’s good.
Silent workers, unseen chore,
Nurture life forevermore.

From earth's embrace, the green is grown,
Tending fields, their role unknown.
Yet in their quiet, endless grind,
The earth's true heart and soul we find.

Underground Canvas

Beneath our feet, an unseen art,
Crafted in the soil's heart.
Layers paint a story deep,
Secrets held where shadows seep.

Colors blend in earthy tones,
Clays and loams, and ancient stones.
Minerals create a hue,
In the dark, a vibrant view.

Webs of roots like brush strokes lie,
Drawing life where life seems dry.
Mycelium threads the forest floor,
Connections unseen yet ever more.

Time the artist, hands unseen,
Shapes the landscape in between.
Buried treasures, life’s remains,
Tell the tale of nature’s gains.

Below, the canvas comes alive,
Earth's own artwork, strives to thrive.
In the dark, the masterpiece,
Of the world, a hidden piece.

Soft Cavity

A whisper through the hollow space,
Where echoes drift in soft embrace.
Gently cradled, dreams entwine,
In the heart where hopes align.

Hidden treasures, tender light,
Blending shadows out of sight.
In this sanctuary of calm repose,
Secrets bloom like unseen prose.

Warmth encircles, close and dear,
Teardrops dry, and fears appear.
Softly spoken words repair,
The fragile soul that hides in there.

Cradle me in silken thread,
Where only sweetest thoughts are fed.
In the cavity, so safe, so mild,
Where peace and truth are reconciled.

Breathing slow in quiet days,
In this haven, time delays.
Gently swaying with the beat,
Of dreams within the soft retreat.

Foundations in the Dark

Beneath the stars, the roots extend,
Foundations in the night defend.
Ancient walls of whispered lore,
Rise from depths where shadows soar.

In the gloom, the heart beats sound,
In silence where the truths are found.
Hidden strength beneath the soil,
Forges life through endless toil.

Midnight sky, with secrets vast,
Guides the dreams of shadows cast.
Deep within the earth's embrace,
Foundations hold to mark their place.

Shrouded forms in twilight's veil,
Reveal the whispers of the tale.
Silent vigils through the night,
Guard the dawn's approaching light.

From the darkness, strength is born,
Rising with the break of morn.
Foundations in the unseen night,
Forge the future, pure and bright.

Veins of the Underbelly

Through the earth, the rivers twine,
Like veins that seek a hidden shrine.
Pulsing with a silent beat,
Bearing tales untold, discreet.

Roots that curl in dark embrace,
Map the underbelly's trace.
Life that thrives in shadows deep,
Safeguarded secrets that they keep.

Liquid pathways, winding streams,
Feeding life's profoundest dreams.
Coursing through the silent lands,
Nurtured by the unseen hands.

Underground, where whispers weave,
Veins of life that never leave.
Hidden from the sunlit gaze,
Moving through the endless maze.

In the dark, where silence sings,
Life's essence flows in subtle strings.
Veins beneath, through secret ways,
Fueling the night's unending praise.

Minstrels of the Mud

In the mire, where shadows play,
Minstrels of the mud convey.
Songs of earth and endless stir,
Life beneath the surface blur.

Hidden voices, rich and low,
Sing where only darkness knows.
Through the soil, their tales impart,
Rhythms of the timeless heart.

Mud-bound poets weave their art,
In the quiet, every part.
Notes of life, both pure and raw,
Humming with nature's awe.

In the muck where roots entwine,
Minstrels sing of the divine.
Murmur of the earth's deep core,
Resonates forevermore.

Listen close and you will hear,
Minstrels of the mud draw near.
From the heart of nature's blend,
Their songs and whispers never end.

Hidden Hallways

In corridors of shadowed grace,
Where whispers dance and shadows chase,
Doors unseen by daylight's face,
Secrets dwell in time's embrace.

Footsteps echo soft and low,
Guiding paths where none may go,
Under moonlight's mystic glow,
Hidden hallways softly flow.

Murmurs of forgotten lore,
Seep from cracks in ancient floor,
Past and present evermore,
Haunting echoes through the door.

Winds of mystery softly blown,
Through these halls of dream unknown,
Silent secrets, gently sewn,
In hidden hallways overgrown.

Lost to ages, yet alive,
Through these shadows, spirits thrive,
Keeping tales of those who strive,
In hidden hallways, tales survive.

Rooted Roads

Winding through the forest deep,
Paths that ancient roots do keep,
There the secrets softly seep,
In the heart where silence sleeps.

Twisting veins of earthen might,
Underneath the leafy light,
Guiding steps by day and night,
Through the woods, an endless rite.

Beneath the canopy so wide,
Where the rooted roads reside,
There the ancient whispers bide,
Nature's course in them confides.

Every step a story told,
To the young from days of old,
Rooted roads, their paths unfold,
Binding earth in gentle hold.

In the forest, shadows blend,
Life and time a river's bend,
Rooted roads that never end,
To the earth our souls they send.

Subtly Buried

Beneath the surface, hidden true,
Treasures lie beyond our view,
In the soil, the earth, the dew,
Subtly buried, born anew.

Secrets held beneath the ground,
Where the quiet peace is found,
Silent whispers all around,
Rhythms of a world profound.

Underneath the meadow's grace,
Resting in a silent place,
Histories in soil's embrace,
Time and space, a hidden trace.

Nature's verses softly blurred,
In the depths, they go unheard,
Subtly buried, like a word,
To the wise, a ciphered bird.

One day time may yield its truth,
Stories of an ancient youth,
Subtly buried, lives uncouth,
Silent wisdom in its sooth.

Earthward Bound

From the heavens to the ground,
Life a cycle, earthward bound,
Roots and reasons intertwined,
Nature's course forever found.

Leaves that flutter, grace the air,
Whispering secrets, words of care,
To the earth they will repair,
Completing life with love to spare.

Mountains high and rivers low,
Crafting paths that ebb and flow,
To the earth our spirits go,
In the soil, new life will grow.

Time's a traveler, always round,
Journey’s end is softly sound,
As our lives in earth are bound,
In its bosom, peace is found.

Through the seasons, we embrace,
Changes holding us in place,
Earthward bound, a tender grace,
In the soil, we find our space.

Beneath the Meadow

Whispers of green where sunlight fades,
In shadows deep, the secret trades,
Roots entwine in silent grace,
Life unseen in that hidden space.

Soft lullabies the soil sings,
To seeds that sleep 'neath nature's wings,
Dreams of blooms and petals bright,
Await the kiss of morning light.

Dewdrops form on tender blades,
A dance of life in coolness wades,
Veils of mist rise, thin and sweet,
Connect the sky with earthy beat.

Ancient songs in silence lie,
Waiting 'til the winds reply,
Beneath the meadow's tranquil flow,
A symphony we scarcely know.

Earthbound Voyages

Silent travelers in the earth,
Questing since their humble birth,
Paths unseen and tales untold,
Earthbound secret, steadfast, bold.

Caverns vast and veins of clay,
Guide their steps in endless sway,
Through the rock and soil they roam,
Seeking out their quiet home.

Wonders lie in worlds below,
Geodes gleam with inner glow,
Whispered winds in tunnels weave,
Songs of ages we perceive.

Voyages that shape the land,
Crafted by a hidden hand,
Earthbound journeys, ever still,
Carving dreams from nature's will.

Undergrowth Mysteries

In the forest's deepest hold,
Mysteries in green unfold,
Fern and moss, a verdant lace,
Draping secrets every place.

Footprints lost to shadow's veil,
Tales of creatures, long and frail,
Whispers flow from root to leaf,
Echoes of a hidden grief.

Mushrooms glow in twilight's hue,
Guardian of secrets true,
In their rings, the fables spin,
Chronicles of life within.

Linger here, where silence reigns,
Cryptic paths in nature's veins,
Undergrowth enshrines a lore,
Ever ancient, evermore.

Underground Serenade

Deep below where sun's rays cease,
Whispers form in timeless peace,
Caves resound with nature's song,
In the dark, they weave along.

Rivers flow in hidden streams,
Carving out the heart's lone dreams,
Echoing through ancient halls,
Mystery in murmured calls.

Crystals hum in secret keys,
Notes that drift upon the breeze,
Symphonies of earth and stone,
Voices meld in undertone.

Quiet realms of endless night,
Serenading pure delight,
Underground, the chorus plays,
Hymns of earth in endless praise.

Echoes Beneath

In silent whispers, shadows creep,
Through caverns deep, where secrets seep.
An ancient song, the earth does keep,
In echoes vast, where spirits weep.

Silver streams in darkness flow,
Where moonlit gleams shall never show.
Deep below, the fires glow,
Among the rocks where crystals grow.

Mystic winds through tunnels wind,
With secrets only night can find.
Phantom thoughts and dreams entwine,
In echoing realms, where time's confined.

Grains of sand in darkened dance,
Through eons past, they find their chance.
Eternal whispers in a trance,
In echoing halls of circumstance.

Footfalls soft on ancient stone,
Where once the gods had kings enthrone.
In shadows, mystery is shown,
And echoes speak, yet all alone.

Brooding Burrows

Beneath the sky where shadows lie,
In burrows deep, the secrets hide.
The roots of trees like rivers wry,
In brooding depths where dreams abide.

Among the soil, the whispers dwell,
In silent calm, where tales do tell.
The ancient ground protects so well,
The stories lost, in shadow’s spell.

Darkness wraps the sleeping ground,
In stillness where no light is found.
The night invades without a sound,
In burrows deep, all things are bound.

Through earthen walls and hidden nooks,
The soil secures all that it took.
In twilight's grasp, the mind it hooks,
To ancient lore and secret books.

Within these depths, a world unknown,
Of life that waits and seeds unsown.
In shadows deep, by stars disowned,
The brooding burrows stand alone.

Chambered Echoes

In caverns vast, the echoes ring,
Where darkness reigns and shadows cling.
A hidden world where voices sing,
And time stands still in chambered spring.

The whispers of the past reside,
In hidden grooves where echoes bide.
Each sound a tale that never died,
In chambered halls where secrets hide.

The silence tells a thousand tales,
Through winding paths and ancient trails.
In darkness where the light prevails,
The chambered echoes softly wail.

Each corridor a mirrored past,
Of moments caught and shadows cast.
In echoes chambered, silence vast,
The future and the present clasped.

The hush of time in stone embraced,
Through ages gone that none can trace.
In chambered echoes, time's own place,
Where whispers of the past erase.

Echoes of the Earth

In valleys deep and mountains high,
The echoes of the earth do lie.
In every breeze that brushes by,
The ancient voices softly sigh.

The rivers flow with whispered grace,
Through canyons carved in time's embrace.
In rushing waves, the earth's own face,
Reflected in the water's chase.

Beneath the stars, the whispers creep,
And in the night, the secrets seep.
The earth in every heartbeat deep,
In echoing tones of silence steep.

The forest hums with life unseen,
In verdant shades of timeless green.
Each leaf a note in nature's theme,
In echoes of the earth's own dream.

From dawn to dusk, the echoes call,
In gentle rain and thunder's thrall.
The earth's own voice, within us all,
In whispers heard, both great and small.

Underground Harmony

In the depths, where shadows sing,
Lies a realm of peaceful night.
Ancient roots in chorus cling,
Veins of earth in silent flight.

Whispers from the soil and clay,
Echoes of forgotten lore.
Nature’s melody at play,
Underground, a secret score.

Muffled hum of life obscure,
Beneath the bustling feet above.
Harmony in darkness pure,
Songs of earth, a hidden love.

Moss and stone in gentle sway,
Underneath this shaded dome.
Timeless symphony on display,
In this subterranean home.

Caverns deep, a tranquil choir,
Crystals glint in muted light.
Underground, the heart’s desire,
Peaceful rhythm of the night.

Underneath the World

Beneath the surface, shadows play,
An underworld, a vast domain.
Mysteries beneath the day,
In earthen halls, by darkness lain.

Tunnels weave a secret tale,
Paths unseen by mortal eyes.
In this maze, the light grows pale,
Whispers of a hidden prize.

Stalactites and crystals gleam,
Guardians of the depths below.
Silent sentinels that dream,
Of the world above, aglow.

Echoes dance on walls of stone,
Reverberating ancient songs.
In these depths, we're not alone,
Where time's pulse gently throngs.

A world beneath, so calm, so still,
Yet full of life, in quiet grace.
Underneath, the earth's own will,
In shadows, finds its rightful place.

Earth's Secret Labyrinth

Winding paths through shadows deep,
A labyrinth of earth's embrace.
Secrets that the stones do keep,
In this hidden, sacred place.

Roots entwined in silent dance,
Through the soil their tendrils weave.
Nature's ancient, whispered trance,
In the darkened dells they leave.

Flickers of a distant glow,
Glowworms light the winding way.
Through the maze where none shall go,
Save those led by night's ballet.

Ancient walls that tell of time,
Stories etched in rock and clay.
Labyrinth in silent rhyme,
Guides the lost who dare to stray.

Deep within this earthen maze,
Where the air is still and cold.
One can find in shadowed haze,
Earth's own secrets, firm and bold.

Dark and Quiet Depths

In the deep where light is thin,
Quiet reigns, a sovereign king.
Whispers soft as whispers win,
In the chambers shadows bring.

Through the dark, a gentle hum,
Nature's lullaby in flow.
In these depths, there lies a drum,
Beating slow, an undertow.

Roots and stones in slumber lie,
Bound by earth in tranquil rest.
In the dark where echoes sigh,
Life proceeds at nature's best.

Veins of water through the rock,
Softly trickle, softly sound.
In this quiet, time unlocks,
Silent secrets underground.

Darkness wraps its velvet shade,
Cradling life in hushed embrace.
In these depths, though light may fade,
Whispered peace finds its true place.